CYBER SHADOWS

A Heist of Passion &

HEM INDER SINGH

With the blessings of God,

This book is:

.

First published in year (2024)

.

This book is a work of fiction and certain concepts discussed in the book are only for informational purposes; any similarities to persons living or dead, or actual events is purely coincidental.

.

.

Any suggestions and feedback are welcome on
heminder1204@gmail.com

****

*Dedicated this book to my parents
-S. Sukhwinderjit Singh & Mrs. Gurdeep Kaur
and my late grandfather S. Parkash Singh Ji.*

----

*All good things happen due to your infinite
blessings and bad due to my own limitations.*

****

CONTENTS

****

PREFACE

Welcome to the "Cyber Shadows" universe, where the distinction between the actual and virtual worlds is hazy and a button click is just as powerful as a sword stroke. It is more important than ever to have guardians of the digital frontier in this ever changing and fast-paced environment.

This book is an account of the incredible trip that TechSpySecure, a group of cybersecurity specialists situated in Mumbai, India, has taken. Their journey, which began as a small startup and culminated in their rise to prominence in the battle against cyber dangers, is one of bravery, tenacity, and unflinching devotion to their goal.

This book's chapters each provide a unique perspective on a different aspect of TechSpySecure's history. From their thrilling encounters with hackers and cybercriminals to their tireless efforts to safeguard critical infrastructure and protect their city from digital harm, the narrative unfolds with a blend of suspense, intrigue, and heart-pounding action.

The ties that are formed amongst TechSpySecure members are what really make this story compelling, even beyond the thrilling cyber fights and heart-pounding chases. They persevere in navigating the intricate network of the digital underworld despite setbacks and triumphs, finding strength in their unyielding solidarity and common goal.

However, the journey is not without its difficulties. TechSpySecure has to negotiate a dangerous and deceitful environment as they take on enemies that are both unexpected and formidable. The risks they face are as varied as they are dangerous, ranging from enigmatic individuals hiding in the shadows of the dark web to state-sponsored enemies using cyberweapons.

And yet, amidst the chaos and uncertainty, there shines a beacon of hope—a reminder that even in the darkest of times, there is always light. For TechSpySecure, that light emanates from their unwavering belief in the power of teamwork, the importance of trust, and the enduring resilience of the human spirit.

As you embark on this journey with TechSpySecure, may you find yourself captivated by their courage, inspired by their resilience, and reminded of the profound importance of vigilance in an increasingly interconnected world. For their story is not just theirs alone—it is a testament to the challenges and opportunities that await us all in this digital age of internet and technology.

CHAPTER 1

THE INCIDENT

Under the afternoon light, the tall towers of Bandra Complex shimmered in the center of Mumbai, the city that never sleeps. Leading cybersecurity company TechSpySecure was a stronghold of technological protection. A tempest was building within its confines. At its core was Arjun Malhotra, a seasoned cybersecurity specialist with ten years of experience.

Arjun was in his mid-thirties, with sharp features and a focus that could cut through steel. His reputation in the industry was impeccable; he was known for his brilliant mind and unwavering commitment to cyber defense. As he navigated through the maze of glass-walled offices, his phone buzzed incessantly with updates and alerts.

The senior management group was waiting for him when he entered the conference room. The tension in the room was palpable. At the head of the table sat Rohit Kapoor, the CEO of TechSpySecure, a man whose usual calm demeanor was now marred by worry lines.

"Arjun, we need you, "Rohit began without preamble. "We have suffered a major breach. Sensitive client data has been compromised, and attackers left no trace."

Arjun's eyes narrowed. "No trace? That's impossible. Every hacker leaves a footprint, however faint."

Rohit handed him a dossier. "This is everything we have so far. Our systems detected unusual activity last night, and by the time we realized it, it was too late."

Arjun flipped through the dossier, his mind racing. The breach was sophisticated, involving multiple layers of **encryption** and **obfuscation**. It was the work of a professional.

"We need to handle this discretly," Rohit continued. " If the media gets wind of this, our reputation will be in ruins. Can you help us, Arjun?"

Arjun nodded, his mind already formulating a plan. "I'll need full access to your systems and the help of my team. We will start immediately."

As he left the conference room, his phone buzzed again. It was a message from Kavya Sharma, an inspector with the Mumbai Cyber Crime Division, an expert in operating M416 gun and his ex-girlfriend. Their breakup had been messy, but they had always respected each other's professional prowess.

"Just heard about TechSpySecure. Are you handling it?" the message read.

"Yes. Need to talk?", he replied.

"Meet me at the usual place in an hour."

The "usual place" was a small café. Kavya was already there, sitting in their usual corner, her laptop open in front of her. She looked up as he approached, her expression unreadable.

"Arjun," she greeted him curtly.

"Kavya," he replied, sitting opposite to her.

"I have been assigned to the TechSpySecure case," she said, getting straight to the point. "I want us to work together on this."

Arjun raised an eyebrow. "You know our history, Kavya. Are you sure that's a good idea?"

"We're professionals, Arjun. We can handle it," she said firmly. "Besides, we need to catch this hacker. They've been on our radar for a while."

Arjun leaned back, considering her words. "What do you know about the attacker?"

"Not much," she admitted. "They go by the alias 'Phantom.' They've been involved in several high-profile cybercrimes across the country, but they always manage to stay one step ahead."

Arjun frowned. Phantom. He had heard the name before, whispered in dark corners of the internet. A ghostly figure, known for their brilliance and elusiveness.

"We need to set aside our differences," Kavya continued. "This is bigger than us."

Arjun nodded slowly. "Agreed. Let's catch this Phantom."

Together, they left the café, their old tensions simmering beneath the surface. As they walked to the TechSpySecure offices, Kavya filled him in on the latest developments.

"We've traced the breach to an unknown server," she explained. "But the trail goes cold there. Whoever did this cover their tracks well using a **proxy server**"

Arjun's mind was already racing with possibilities. "We'll need to conduct a thorough forensic analysis of the systems. There's always a footprint, no matter how small."

They arrived at TechSpySecure, where Rohit was waiting for them. He looked relieved to see Kavya, knowing her reputation for cracking tough cases.

"We'll start with a complete analysis of the breach," Arjun said. "Kavya, can you get us access to the police cyber forensics lab?"

"Already done," she replied. "I've also called in a couple of my best officers to assist."

Arjun turned to Rohit. "I need a secure room where we can work without interruptions."

Rohit nodded and led them to a conference room that had been converted into a temporary command center. Arjun set up his laptop and connected to the network, his fingers flying over the keyboard as he began his analysis.

Kavya watched him work, her respect for his skills grudgingly resurfacing. Despite their personal history, she knew he was the best in the business.

Hours passed as they delved deeper into the breach. Arjun's expertise combined with Kavya's investigative skills made them a formidable team. They uncovered clues that hinted at a highly sophisticated attack, using techniques that only a handful of hackers in the world could execute.

As the night wore on, Arjun's phone buzzed with a call from one of his team members. It was Riya Aggarwal, a brilliant hacker he had mentored years ago. She now led a group of young hackers known as the Cyber Squad.

"Arjun, I heard about the breach," she said without preamble. "Do you need help?"

"Riya, I was just about to call you," Arjun replied. "We're dealing with Phantom. I could use all the help I can get."

"I'll assemble the team and be there in an hour," she promised.

True to her word, Riya arrived with Ankit and Tara, her top teammates. Ankit was a **social engineering** expert, while Tara specialized in **penetration testing**. They were young, but their skills were unmatched.

"Alright, team," Arjun said, briefing them on the situation. "We're dealing with a highly skilled hacker who goes by the alias Phantom. Our first priority is to trace the origin of the breach and secure the compromised data."

Riya nodded. "Let's get to work."

With the Cyber Squad on board, their efforts intensified. They used a variety of tools and techniques, from Nmap for network scanning to Wireshark for packet analysis. Each clue they uncovered brought them closer to Phantom, but the hacker was always one step ahead.

As they worked, Kavya noticed a pattern in the data. "Look at this," she said, pointing to a series of timestamps. "The breaches all occurred at the same time every night."

Arjun frowned, studying the data. "You're right. That could be our window of opportunity. If we can predict when Phantom will strike next, we can set a trap."

They devised a plan to create a honeypot – a decoy system designed to attract cyber attackers. It would appear vulnerable, but in reality, it was a carefully monitored trap.

The next night, they set their plan in motion. The tension in the room was palpable as they waited for Phantom to take the bait. Minutes ticked by, feeling like hours.

Then, it happened. An alert flashed on Arjun's screen. Phantom had taken the bait.

"He's in," Arjun said, with his voice tense. "Everyone, stay sharp."

They watched as Phantom navigated the decoy system, probing its defences. The hacker was skilled, but Arjun and his team were ready. They traced Phantom's movements, capturing every detail.

Finally, they had a breakthrough. "I've got **an IP address**," Riya said with excitement, "It's coming from a server farm on the outskirts of the city."

Kavya immediately relayed the information to her team. "We've got a location. Move out!"

As the police prepared to raid the server farm, Arjun and his team continued to monitor Phantom's activities. They knew this was their best chance to catch the elusive hacker.

The raid was swift and efficient. Kavya led her team with precision, apprehending several individuals who were part of Phantom's network. But Phantom himself remained elusive, slipping away in the chaos.

Back at TechSpySecure, Arjun and Kavya reviewed the captured data. They had made significant progress, but the mastermind was still at large.

"This isn't over," Kavya said, determination in her eyes. "We'll catch him."

Arjun nodded. "We're getting closer. He can't hide forever."

As they prepared for the next phase of their investigation, Arjun couldn't help but feel a sense of anticipation. The game was on, and he was ready to face Phantom head-on.

The hunt had only just begun.

****

CHAPTER 2

A MYSTERIOUS LEAD

The following morning, the team at TechSpySecure was already bustling with activity. The coffee machines were working overtime, and the faint hum of computers filled the air. Arjun sat at his makeshift command centre, analysing the data they had gathered from the previous night's raid. The atmosphere was charged with a mix of exhaustion and determination.

Kavya walked in, carrying two steaming cups of coffee. She handed one to Arjun, who accepted it with a grateful nod. Despite the long night, her sharp eyes revealed an unyielding determination. "Any new leads?" she asked, sitting beside him.

Arjun took a sip of his coffee and pointed to his screen. "We've been combing through the data from the server farm. Most of it is encrypted, but we found something interesting. An email chain with several attachments, all password-protected."

Kavya leaned in; her curiosity piqued. "Can you crack it?"

Arjun's lips curled into a confident smirk. "Already on it. I've got Ankit working on it. He's our social engineering expert – if anyone can figure out the password, it's him."

Just then, Ankit, a wiry young man with an infectious grin, entered the room, a look of triumph on his face. "Got it!"

he announced, holding up a USB drive. "The password was a combination of dates – significant events in the life of someone named 'Nisha'. Looks like Phantom has a personal connection."

Arjun plugged the drive into his laptop and opened the files. They revealed a series of blueprints and schematics, detailing a complex cyber heist targeting several major financial institutions. Kavya's eyes widened as she scanned the documents. "This is huge. If Phantom pulls this off, the economic fallout would be catastrophic."

Arjun nodded grimly. "We need to stop him before he can execute his plan. But first, we need to understand his motives and his connections."

Riya, who had been quietly observing from the corner of the room, stepped forward. "I did some digging. 'Nisha' is a known alias in the hacking community, often associated with Phantom. It's possible she's more than just an accomplice."

Kavya frowned. "We need to find her. She might be the key to locating Phantom."

Using their combined resources, the team began an intensive search for Nisha. They scoured the dark web, analysed financial transactions, and monitored communication channels. Hours turned into days, but their efforts were met with little success.

One evening, as Arjun sat in the dimly lit office, pouring over yet another set of logs, Kavya walked in, her expression unreadable. "We've got a lead," she said, holding up a piece of paper. "An informant came forward. Claims to know Nisha and her whereabouts."

Arjun's interest was immediately piqued. "Where is she?"

Kavya hesitated. "It's a trap, Arjun. The informant wants a meeting at an abandoned factory in Navi Mumbai. It screams setup."

Arjun leaned back, considering their options. "We don't have much choice. If this lead pans out, it could be our best chance to catch Phantom. We'll go in prepared."

The next night, under the cover of darkness, Arjun, Kavya, and a small team of officers made their way to the designated meeting spot. The factory was a decaying relic of the past, its broken windows and rusted machinery creating a dirty atmosphere.

Kavya signalled her team to spread out and take positions. She and Arjun moved cautiously through the shadows, their senses on high alert. As they approached the centre of the factory, they saw a figure standing in the dim light.

"Nisha?" Kavya called out, her voice echoing through the empty space.

The figure turned, revealing a young woman with striking features and a wary expression. "Who's asking?" she replied, her voice tinged with defence.

Arjun stepped forward, his gaze steady. "We're here to talk. We know about your connection to Phantom."

Nisha's eyes flickered with recognition and a hint of fear. "You don't understand. It's not what you think!"

Before she could say more, a sudden sound of footsteps echoed through the factory. Arjun and Kavya turned just in time to see a group of masked figures closing in on them. It was an **ambush**.

Kavya reacted swiftly, drawing her weapon and taking cover behind a stack of crates. Arjun followed suit, his mind racing with strategies. The masked figures opened fire, bullets ricocheting off the metal surfaces around them.

Amid the chaos, Nisha made a run for it. Arjun cursed under his breath. "We can't let her escape!" he shouted to Kavya.

Kavya nodded, covering him as he sprinted after Nisha. The factory became a battleground, with gunfire and shouts filling the air. Arjun pushed forward, his heart pounding as he closed the distance between him and Nisha.

Just as he reached her, one of the masked figures appeared, blocking his path. The assailant lunged at Arjun, but he was ready. Using his combat training, he deflected the attack and delivered a swift blow, incapacitating the attacker.

Arjun grabbed Nisha's arm. "We're not your enemies," he said urgently. "We need your help to stop Phantom."

Nisha hesitated, fear and uncertainty warring in her eyes. Finally, she nodded. "Alright. But you need to protect me. Phantom won't stop until I'm dead."

Arjun's grip tightened. "We will. Now let's get out of here."

With Kavya and the officers providing cover, they made their way out of the factory. As they emerged into the night, Arjun knew they had taken a crucial step forward. Nisha held the key to unravelling Phantom's plan, and they were determined to see it through.

The game was getting more dangerous, but Arjun was ready to face whatever came next. The hunt for Phantom was far from over, and the stakes had never been higher.

****

CHAPTER 3

THE WEB OF DECEPTION

Arjun, Kavya, and Nisha hastily departed the derelict factory, the echoes of their narrow escape still fresh in their minds. The night air was thick with tension as they retreated to TechSpySecure's fortified headquarters, where Nisha would be safe and the team could regroup. In the dimly lit war room, surrounded by monitors and the hum of servers, they prepared to uncover the next layer of Phantom's intricate scheme.

Nisha, visibly shaken but resolute, began to divulge her knowledge about Phantom. "He's not just a hacker," she started, her voice barely above a whisper. "He's a master manipulator, weaving a web of deception that spans continents. His network is vast, and his motives... personal."

Arjun leaned in, his analytical mind racing. "Why personal? What drives him?"

Nisha hesitated, then took a deep breath. "Phantom, or as I know him, Vikram, was once a respected cybersecurity expert. We were... close, partners in many ways. But he changed after a series of betrayals by those he trusted. His actions now are driven by a twisted sense of justice and revenge."

Kavya, ever the pragmatist, interjected. "We need to know his next move. These blueprints we found suggest a major heist targeting financial institutions. How can we stop him?"

Nisha's eyes flashed with determination. "He'll strike during the annual financial summit in Mumbai. It's the perfect opportunity for him to cause maximum disruption."

Arjun and Kavya exchanged a glance. The summit was in three days, giving them precious little time to prepare. They needed to anticipate Phantom's every move and counteract his strategy with precision.

The team worked tirelessly, utilizing every resource at their disposal. Riya, Ankit, and Tara dug deep into the dark web, tracing Phantom's digital footprint and identifying his associates. They discovered a series of cryptic messages and transactions pointing to the acquisition of high-end hacking tools and insider information.

As they pieced together the clues, a clearer picture emerged. Phantom planned to infiltrate the summit's security systems, manipulate the financial markets, and siphon off billions in mere minutes. It was an **audacious** plan, but not beyond his capabilities.

To counter this, Arjun devised a multi-layered defence strategy. They would secure the summit's network with advanced encryption, set up intrusion detection systems, and deploy **honeypots** to lure Phantom into revealing himself. Additionally, Kavya coordinated with local law enforcement and international cybercrime agencies to ensure they had boots on the ground.

In the midst of this frenetic activity, the personal dynamics between the team members added another layer of complexity. The old tensions between Arjun and Kavya resurfaced, fuelled by their shared history and the high-stakes nature of their mission. Meanwhile, a tentative alliance formed between Nisha and Kavya, both understanding the need to put aside personal grievances for the greater good.

On the eve of the summit, Arjun found himself alone on the rooftop of TechSpySecure's, gazing out over the city that he had sworn to protect. Nisha joined him, her presence a silent reminder of the personal stakes involved.

"You still care about him, don't you?" Arjun asked softly.

Nisha nodded, her eyes reflecting the city lights. "I do. But I can't let him destroy everything in his quest for vengeance."

Arjun placed a reassuring hand on her shoulder. "We'll stop him. Together."

As the summit began, the tension was palpable. Every attendee, every transaction, every piece of data was a potential target. Arjun, Kavya, and the Cyber Squad were on high alert, monitoring every possible vector of attack.

When the breach finally occurred, it was a coordinated assault on multiple fronts. Phantom's digital presence was felt across the network, attempting to bypass their defences with unprecedented skill. But Arjun and his team were ready. They countered each move with precision, isolating the threats and neutralizing the breaches.

In a dramatic confrontation, they traced Phantom's signal to a hidden server farm on the outskirts of the city. Kavya led a tactical team to the location, storming the facility with military precision. There, in a high-stakes showdown, they apprehended Vikram, the man behind the mask.

Back at TechSpySecure, as the dust settled, the team reflected on their victory. It was a hard-fought battle, one that tested their skills and their resolve. Arjun and Kavya shared a moment of quiet reflection, acknowledging the bond that had helped them through.

Nisha, standing apart, watched as Vikram was taken away. She knew that the battle against cyber threats was far from over, but she had found allies she could trust.

In the heart of Mumbai, under the shadow of towering skyscrapers, the cyber warriors of TechSpySecure had proven that even in the face of relentless digital darkness, the light of determination and collaboration could prevail.

****

CHAPTER 4

SHADOWS OF THE PAST

Mumbai's famous skyline was illuminated by the early sun's golden radiance. The TechSpySecure headquarters was buzzing with a mixture of relief and tiredness following the events of the previous night. Even though he was tired, Arjun had a fresh feeling of purpose. Phantom understood that the battle was far from finished, even though they had foiled his immediate plans. Even though Vikram was in detention and would eventually face justice for his crimes, the intricacies of his network continued to cast a shadow over everything.

Arjun entered the command center, where members of his team were working hard. The sound of voices murmuring and computers humming filled the air. Kavya was in the middle, liaising with forensic experts and police enforcement. She turned as Arjun approached, a look of determination in her eyes.

"Morning," Arjun greeted her. "How's Vikram?"

Kavya sighed. "Uncooperative, as expected. He's not giving up any information about his network or future plans. We need to find another way to break through his defences."

Arjun nodded, understanding the challenge. "We need to dig deeper into his past. There might be clues about his motivations and vulnerabilities. If we can understand what drives him, we might find a way to get him to talk."

As they discussed their next steps, Nisha entered the room, her presence a stark reminder of the personal stakes involved. She had barely slept, her eyes red-rimmed but resolute.

"I want to talk to him," she said. "He might open up to me."

Kavya and Arjun exchanged a glance. It was a risky move, but Nisha's connection to Vikram could be the key to unravelling his secrets.

"Alright," Arjun agreed. "But we'll be monitoring the conversation closely. We can't afford any shocks or surprises."

They escorted Nisha to the secure interrogation room where Vikram was being held. The room was stark and sterile, a single table and two chairs under the harsh fluorescent lights. Vikram sat, shackled, his expression impassive as Nisha entered.

"Nisha," he greeted her with a hint of a smile. "I wondered how long it would take for you to come."

She sat across from him, her eyes meeting his. "Why, Vikram? Why go down this path?"

He leaned back, studying her. "You wouldn't understand. It's about more than just the money or the thrill. It's about justice, about making those who betrayed me pay."

Nisha's eyes softened with a mix of pity and frustration. "This isn't justice, Vikram. It's destruction. You're hurting innocent people."

Vikram's expression hardened. "Innocent? They're all complicit in a system that's broken. I'm just levelling the playing field."

As Nisha continued to probe, Arjun and Kavya listened intently from the observation room. It was clear that Vikram's sense of betrayal ran deep, driving his actions with a fervour that bordered on **fanaticism**. They needed a different approach to reach him.

Arjun had an idea. "We need to show him that there's another way, that his skills can be used for good. Maybe then he'll see reason."

Kavya nodded thoughtfully. "But how do we convince someone so entrenched in their own narrative?"

"We need to find someone he respects," Arjun suggested. "Someone from his past who can appeal to the part of him that still believes in doing the right thing."

Their research led them to Dr. Anjali Rao, a renowned cybersecurity expert who had once mentored Vikram. She was now a professor at a prestigious university, respected for her ethical stance on cybersecurity and her innovative research.

Arjun and Kavya reached out to Dr. Rao, explaining the situation and their hope that she could help. She agreed to meet with them, recognizing the gravity of the situation.

The following day, Dr. Rao arrived at TechSpySecure. She was a dignified woman in her fifties, with sharp eyes and an air of quiet authority. She listened as Arjun and Kavya outlined Vikram's descent into hacking and his current predicament.

"I remember Vikram well," she said thoughtfully. "He was one of my brightest students, but also one of the most troubled. His brilliance was always tempered by a deep-seated anger and a sense of injustice. If he's gone down this path, it's because he believes it's the only way to make things right."

"Can you reach him?" Kavya asked. "Can you make him see that there's another way?"

Dr. Rao nodded slowly. "I can try. But it will take more than words. He needs to see that his actions have consequences, and that there are better ways to use his talents."

They arranged for Dr. Rao to meet with Vikram in the same interrogation room. This time, the atmosphere was different. Vikram's eyes widened in surprise as his former mentor entered. He stood, the chains clinking softly, a flicker of respect in his gaze.

"Dr. Rao," he greeted her, his voice subdued. "I didn't expect to see you here."

She smiled gently, taking a seat. "Vikram, you've come a long way since our days at the university. But this path you've chosen… it's not what I taught you."

He looked away, a shadow crossing his face. "The world isn't as simple as you think, Dr. Rao. Sometimes, you have to break the rules to fix what's broken."

Dr. Rao leaned forward, her eyes piercing. "But at what cost, Vikram? You're destroying lives, undermining the very foundations of society. There's always a choice, and there's always a better way."

Their conversation was long and intense, touching on their shared history, Vikram's sense of betrayal, and the ethical dilemmas that had led him to his current predicament. Slowly, the walls Vikram had built around himself began to crack.

"You have a gift, Vikram," Dr. Rao said softly. "A brilliant mind capable of incredible things. But using it to tear down instead of build-up is a waste of your potential. You can still make a difference, but you need to choose a different path."

Vikram's shoulders slumped, the weight of his actions finally sinking in. "What if it's too late? What if I can't go back?"

Dr. Rao reached out, placing a comforting hand on his. "It's never too late to change, Vikram. But you have to want it. You have to be willing to face the consequences and make amends."

Back in the observation room, Arjun and Kavya watched with bated breath. They could see the struggle in Vikram's eyes, the internal battle between his desire for vengeance and the realization of what he had become.

Finally, Vikram looked up at Dr. Rao, his expression one of weary resignation. "I'll cooperate. I'll help you dismantle my network and stop the heist."

Relief washed over Arjun and Kavya. It was a small victory, but a significant one. They had managed to reach Vikram and turn him from an enemy into a reluctant ally.

As the team prepared to act on Vikram's information, Arjun knew that the fight against cyber threats was far from over. But they had made progress, and with Vikram's help, they stood a chance of dismantling his network and preventing future attacks.

****

CHAPTER 5

THE HIDDEN FORTRESS

The Mumbai skyline twinkled with countless lights as Arjun, Kavya, and their team prepared for their next move. With Vikram's cooperation, they now had critical intel on the locations and operations of his sprawling hacker network. The stakes were higher than ever, and the team's determination was palpable.

Arjun gathered everyone in the command center, the room buzzing with anticipation. "We've identified several key nodes in Phantom's network," he began, referring to Vikram by his hacker alias. "Our primary target is a hidden server farm located in a remote part of Maharashtra. This facility is the nerve center of his operations."

Kavya pointed to a detailed map on the screen, highlighting the server farm's location. "It's heavily guarded, both physically and digitally. We'll need a different approach—an elite team on the ground and a simultaneous cyber **assault** to disable their defences."

The plan was ambitious, but the team had faced high-risk operations before. Arjun outlined the roles: Kavya would lead the ground team, including a contingent of SWAT officers, while Arjun would oversee the cyber assault from their headquarters.

As they finalized their strategy, Nisha approached Arjun. "I want to help," she said, her voice steady. "I know Vikram's methods better than anyone. I can guide you through his digital defenses and strategies."

Arjun hesitated but saw the determination in her eyes. "Alright," he agreed. "But you stay here with me. It's going to be dangerous."

That night, as the city slept, TechSpySecure mobilized its forces. Kavya and her team boarded unmarked vehicles, heading towards the remote location under the cover of darkness. Arjun, Nisha, and the cyber squad remained at the command center, preparing for the digital **onslaught**.

Kavya's convoy navigated through narrow, winding roads; the tension palpable. They arrived at the outskirts of the server farm, a nondescript building surrounded by dense forest. Kavya signalled her team to disembark and take up positions.

"Remember," she whispered into her comms. "Stealth is key. We can't afford to alert them prematurely."

Meanwhile, back at the command center, Arjun and Nisha were deep into the cyber battle. Vikram had designed an intricate web of defenses, but Nisha's insights proved invaluable. She guided Arjun's team through layers of firewalls, encryption, and decoy systems.

"We're in," Arjun announced, his eyes fixed on the screen. "Initiating the main breach. Kavya, you're clear to move in."

Kavya acknowledged, signalling her team to advance. They moved with military precision, neutralizing guards and bypassing security systems. As they breached the facility, Kavya led them through dimly lit corridors towards the server room.

In the command center, Arjun and Nisha hit a snag. A sudden surge in defensive protocols threatened to lock them out. "He's got a fail-safe," Nisha warned. "We need to disable it, or it'll trigger a self-destruct sequence."

Arjun's mind raced as he analyzed the data. "We need to isolate the central processing unit. It's the only way to stop the fail-safe."

Nisha worked furiously, her fingers flying over the keyboard. "I've found it," she said, her voice tinged with urgency. "But it's protected by a biometric lock. We need Vikram's input."

Arjun's heart sank. They had Vikram in custody, but getting him to cooperate in real-time under these circumstances was risky. He made a quick decision. "Patch Vikram through."

Vikram's face appeared on the monitor; his expression unreadable. "You need my help," he stated, a hint of satisfaction in his voice.

"We don't have time for games," Arjun snapped. "Give us the override code."

Vikram sighed, leaning back. "I'll help, but you need to understand—shutting down this server farm won't stop everything. There are more nodes, more plans in motion."

"Just give us the code," Arjun insisted, his patience wearing thin.

Vikram relented, providing the necessary input. As Nisha implemented the override, Arjun turned his attention back to Kavya. "We've got the fail-safe disabled. You're good to go."

Kavya and her team reached the server room, a cavernous space filled with rows of humming machines. They quickly planted explosives at strategic points, ready to bring the entire operation down.

"Charges set," Kavya reported. "Explosion in three minutes."

As the team made their way out, the facility's alarms blared. Their stealth approach had been compromised. "Move, move, move!" Kavya shouted, leading her team through a hail of gunfire.

In the command center, Arjun and Nisha watched the live feed, their hearts pounding. The ground team's extraction was perilous, but they managed to evade the guards and reach their vehicles.

"Kavya, status?" Arjun called out, his voice tense.

"We're clear," she replied, breathless but triumphant. "Detonating in ten."

A series of explosions rocked the facility, and the feed went dark. The team had successfully neutralized the server farm, delivering a significant blow to Phantom's network.

As Kavya's convoy returned, Arjun turned to Nisha. "We did it. But Vikram's right. This is just the beginning. We need to dismantle his entire network."

Nisha nodded, her resolve unwavering. "I'm with you. We'll see this through to the end."

The victory was bittersweet. They had struck a major blow, but the war against Phantom was far from over. The shadows of his influence still lingered, and they had to be vigilant.

Later that night, as the team debriefed, Arjun couldn't shake the feeling that Vikram had more tricks up his sleeve. The man was a master strategist, always thinking several steps ahead.

"Kavya," he said, as they reviewed the mission. "We need to be prepared for retaliation. Vikram won't take this loss lightly."

Kavya nodded her expression seriously. "Agreed. We need to strengthen our defences and stay one step ahead."

The atmosphere in the room was charged with a mixture of exhaustion and determination. They had faced incredible odds and emerged victorious, but they knew the path ahead would be fraught with challenges.

Arjun gazed out the window, the city lights reflecting his thoughts. The battle against Phantom was a test of their skills, their resolve, and their unity. As long as they stood together, they believed they could overcome any obstacle.

In the heart of the digital age, the warriors of TechSpySecure prepared for the next chapter of their relentless pursuit. The shadows of the past might linger, but they were ready to face whatever came their way, united in their mission to protect the world from the unseen threats lurking in the depths of cyberspace.

****

CHAPTER 6

THE DIGITAL CHESSBOARD

The dawn following the raid on Vikram's server farm was tinged with a sense of uneasy triumph at TechSpySecure headquarters. They had dealt a significant blow to Phantom's operations, but the digital war was far from over. Arjun, Kavya, and their team knew that this was merely a skirmish in a larger conflict.

In the command center, the team reviewed the data they had recovered from the server farm. Arjun's sharp eyes scanned the lines of code, searching for patterns, while Kavya coordinated with law enforcement and intelligence agencies to follow up on leads. Nisha, a crucial ally now, worked alongside them, her insights into Vikram's methods proving invaluable.

"We've decrypted some of the data," Arjun announced, his voice cutting through the tension. "It looks like Vikram was planning multiple attacks. Financial institutions, government databases, even some critical infrastructure. This wasn't just about money—it's about destabilizing entire systems."

Kavya frowned, her mind racing. "We need to identify his next targets and fortify their defences. Can we trace his network back to its origin?"

Arjun shook his head. "He's clever. His network is decentralized, using proxies and false trails. But there's a pattern here. If we can figure out his logic, we might predict his moves."

Nisha leaned over, pointing to a cluster of data points. "These coordinates—they match locations of major tech companies and datacenters. He's targeting the backbone of our digital infrastructure."

Arjun's eyes widened. "If he takes those down, it could cripple our economy and security. We need to warn them and prepare countermeasures."

As the team sprang into action, fortifying the defenses of potential targets and coordinating with cyber defense units across the country, an encrypted message appeared on Arjun's screen. It was from Vikram.

"You think you've won a battle, Arjun," the message read. "But this is a chess game, and you've merely taken a pawn. The king is still in play, and your moves are predictable."

Arjun's jaw tightened. "He's taunting us. He wants us to react impulsively."

Kavya, reading over his shoulder, narrowed her eyes. "Then we need to stay ahead of him. Let's think like he does let's anticipate his strategy."

The team delved into a psychological profile of Vikram, piecing together his history, motivations, and likely next moves. They consulted with Dr. Anjali Rao again, seeking her insights into Vikram's mindset.

"Vikram always thrived on challenges," Dr. Rao explained. "He sees this as a game where he can outwit his opponents. But he's also driven by a need for recognition. If you can disrupt his narrative, you might force him to make a mistake."

Inspired, Arjun devised a plan. They would set a trap, creating a false trail that would lure Vikram into a vulnerable position. Using a combination of honeypots—decoy systems designed to attract and monitor hackers—and misinformation, they aimed to make Vikram believe he had found a weak link in their network.

As the team set up the digital trap, the tension mounted. Every keystroke, every decision had to be precise. Arjun and Nisha worked closely, their minds in sync as they crafted the intricate web.

"Everything's in place," Arjun said, his voice steady despite the pressure. "Now we wait."

Hours turned into a day, the team remaining vigilant. Finally, a breach alert flashed on Arjun's screen. Vikram had taken the bait.

"He's in," Nisha confirmed, her eyes fixed on the monitors. "He's accessing the decoy system."

Arjun's heart raced. "We need to keep him engaged long enough to trace his location. Stay sharp, everyone."

As Vikram navigated the decoy system, Arjun and his team monitored his every move, subtly guiding him deeper into the trap. They watched as he attempted to breach the false security layers, his digital fingerprints becoming clearer.

"We've got a lock on his location," Kavya announced, her voice tinged with excitement. "It's a mobile setup—he's on the move, but we've got him."

Arjun coordinated with law enforcement, dispatching a tactical unit to intercept Vikram's mobile command center. The team moved swiftly, converging on the target location—a van parked in an industrial area on the outskirts of Mumbai.

The confrontation was intense. Vikram, realizing he had been trapped, attempted to erase his data and flee. But the tactical unit, backed by TechSpySecure's real-time intelligence, apprehended him before he could escape.

Back at headquarters, the team watched the live feed of Vikram being taken into custody. There was a collective sigh of relief, but also a recognition of the battles still ahead.

Arjun turned to Nisha, who looked both relieved and troubled. "We've stopped him, for now. But he's right—

it's a chess game. And there are more pieces on the board."

Nisha nodded, her eyes reflecting a mixture of determination and weariness. "We'll be ready. Whatever comes next, we'll face it together."

As the team regrouped, Arjun couldn't shake the feeling that this was just the beginning. Vikram's network was vast, and others would rise to take his place. The digital battlefield was constantly evolving, and they had to stay ahead.

In the quiet moments after the storm, Arjun looked out over the city. The lights of Mumbai shimmered, a reminder of the lives they were protecting. The fight against cyber threats was relentless, but so was their resolve.

The warriors of TechSpySecure had proven their mettle, but they knew the journey was far from over. The shadows of the digital world were ever-present, and the next challenge could come from anywhere.

As dawn broke, casting a new light over the city, Arjun and his team prepared for whatever lay ahead. They were united, driven by a common purpose, ready to defend against the unseen threats that lurked in the depths of cyberspace.

****

CHAPTER 7

ECHOES OF BETRAYAL

In the aftermath of their latest victory against Phantom, the atmosphere at TechSpySecure was a mix of relief and tension. Arjun, Kavya, and their team knew that while they had thwarted one threat, the world of cyber warfare was an ever-shifting battleground. As they regrouped in the command center, the air crackled with anticipation of what might come next.

Arjun glanced around at his team; their faces weary but determined. "We've dealt a significant blow to Phantom's network," he began, his voice steady. "But we can't afford to let our guard down. We need to stay vigilant and be ready for whatever he throws at us next."

Kavya nodded in agreement, her eyes scanning the room. "We also need to consider the possibility of insider threats. Phantom has proven himself to be resourceful. He could have allies within our own ranks."

The suggestion hung in the air, a sobering reminder of the complexity of their situation. Arjun trusted his team implicitly, but in the world of **espionage** and betrayal, trust could be a dangerous commodity.

As they delved deeper into their analysis of Phantom's network, a red flag appeared on one of the monitors. An unauthorized access attempt had been detected on TechSpySecure's internal servers.

"Trace it," Arjun commanded, his senses on high alert.

The team sprang into action, tracing the intrusion back to its source. It led to an employee's terminal—a young programmer named Aryan, whose skills had impressed Arjun when he first joined the team.

Arjun's heart sank. Aryan had been one of their brightest talents, eager to learn and eager to prove himself. But now, it seemed he had fallen prey to Phantom's influence.

"We need to bring him in," Kavya said, her voice grim. "We can't risk him leaking sensitive information to Phantom and become our **trojan.**"

Aryan was located in his cubicle, his eyes glued to his computer screen. He looked up as Arjun and Kavya approached, a flicker of guilt crossing his face.

"Aryan, what are you doing?" Arjun asked, his tone firm but not accusatory.

Aryan hesitated, his fingers hovering over the keyboard. "I... I don't know," he stammered. "I was just following orders."

Arjun's heart sank. It was a familiar refrain; one he had heard from countless others who had been drawn into Phantom's web. The allure of power, of belonging, was a potent force, capable of clouding even the most rational minds.

"We can help you, Aryan," Kavya said, her voice soft but determined. "But you need to tell us everything you know. Who contacted you? What did they want?"

Aryan's shoulders slumped; the weight of his betrayal evident. "It was a woman," he confessed. "She said she was a recruiter for a prestigious tech firm, offering me a job with better pay and benefits. But there were conditions—I had to provide them with information about TechSpySecure's operations."

Arjun's jaw clenched. It was a classic tactic, exploiting the vulnerabilities of ambitious young professionals to gain access to sensitive information. But, it also spoke to a deeper betrayal—a betrayal of trust, of loyalty, of the ideals they fought to uphold.

"We need to find out who this woman is," Arjun said, his voice tinged with anger. "And we need to shut down this recruitment operation before it does any more damage."

With Aryan's cooperation, they were able to trace the communication back to a burner phone registered to a shell corporation with ties to Phantom's network. It was a dead end, but it confirmed their suspicions—Phantom was operating on multiple fronts, using every tool at his disposal to undermine their efforts.

As they debriefed the incident, Arjun couldn't shake the feeling of unease that settled over him. The betrayal of one of their own was a stark reminder of the dangers they faced, both from external threats and from within.

"We need to tighten our security protocols," Arjun said, his voice determined. "We can't afford any more lapses in judgment. The stakes are too high."

Kavya nodded in agreement, her eyes reflecting the steely resolve that Arjun had come to rely on. "We'll conduct a thorough review of our personnel and procedures. We can't let Phantom's influence infiltrate our ranks."

As the team dispersed to carry out their tasks, Arjun found himself alone in the command center, the weight of their mission pressing down on him. The battle against Phantom was far from over, and the echoes of betrayal would linger long after the conflict had ended.

In the digital age, trust was a fragile commodity, easily broken and difficult to repair. But Arjun knew that as long as they stood together, united in their purpose, they could weather any storm.

As he gazed out over the city, the lights of Mumbai twinkling in the distance, Arjun renewed his vow to protect his team, his colleagues, and his city from the insidious threats that lurked in the shadows of cyberspace. They were the guardians of a new frontier, tasked with defending against adversaries who operated with impunity in the digital realm.

But as Arjun reflected on the challenges they faced, he also drew strength from the unwavering dedication of his team. Despite the betrayals and the constant threat of attack, they remained steadfast in their commitment to safeguarding the digital infrastructure of their nation.

In the days that followed, TechSpySecure implemented rigorous security measures, conducting thorough background checks on all personnel and implementing enhanced encryption protocols to protect their data. They also intensified their efforts to dismantle Phantom's network, working tirelessly to track down his allies and disrupt his operations.

As they delved deeper into the murky world of cybercrime, Arjun couldn't help but feel a sense of urgency. The longer Phantom remained at large, the greater the risk to their security—and the security of the world at large. They needed to stop him, once and for all, before he could unleash chaos on an larger scale.

But even as they pursued their relentless pursuit of justice, Arjun couldn't shake the feeling of unease that gnawed at him. Phantom was a formidable adversary, cunning and resourceful, and he knew that their next encounter could be their most challenging yet.

As he prepared to face the trials that lay ahead, Arjun found solace in the knowledge that he was not alone. With Kavya, Nisha, and the rest of his team by his side, he knew that they could overcome any obstacle, no matter how daunting.

And so, as the sun set over Mumbai and the city settled into the quiet of the night, Arjun steeled himself for the battles yet to come. For in the world of cyber warfare, the line between victory and defeat was razor-thin, and the echoes of betrayal lingered like shadows in the darkness. But with courage, determination, and unwavering resolve, Arjun and his team were ready to face whatever challenges awaited them, for they were the defenders of the digital realm, the guardians of a new era, and they would stop at nothing to protect their world from those who sought to do it harm.

****

CHAPTER 8

SHADOWS IN THE DARK

The night had settled over Mumbai, its skyline a glittering tapestry against the inky black sky. Inside TechSpySecure headquarters, a sense of uneasy calm permeated the air. Aryan's betrayal had been a stark reminder of the vulnerabilities they faced, and Arjun, Kavya, and their team were more vigilant than ever.

It was 10 o'clock, Arjun stood by the large window in the command center, his eyes scanning the city's lights below. His mind was a whirlwind of strategies and potential threats. Kavya approached, her expression mirroring his resolve.

"We've made progress, but Phantom is still out there," Kavya said, her voice firm. "We need to stay proactive, anticipate his next move."

Arjun nodded. "Absolutely. We need to disrupt his operations before he can strike again. Let's focus on his key operatives. If we can dismantle his network, we can weaken his grip."

The team assembled in the briefing room early the next morning. Arjun, Kavya, and Nisha stood before a large screen displaying profiles of Phantom's top lieutenants. Among them was Shalini Desai, a brilliant coder known for her encryption expertise.

"Shalini is a priority target," Arjun announced. "She's one of Phantom's best. If we can capture her, we can gain critical intel and possibly turn her against him."

Kavya outlined the plan to locate and apprehend Shalini. "She operates out of a fortified facility in Bengaluru. We'll need stealth and precision. This has to be a clean extraction."

The tension was palpable as the team prepared for the mission. Each member knew their role and the importance of executing it flawlessly. Failure was not an option.

As night fell, the team moved out, their convoy slicing through the bustling city streets. The approach to the facility was shrouded in darkness, the air thick with anticipation. Kavya and the tactical unit took the lead, while Arjun and Nisha monitored the operation from a mobile command center.

Inside the facility, Shalini was already aware of their presence. Her sophisticated security systems had detected the breach, and she was racing to erase sensitive data. Kavya's team infiltrated swiftly, neutralizing guards and bypassing security protocols with practiced efficiency.

They reached Shalini's control room just as she was about to initiate a data wipe. Kavya and her team burst in, weapons trained on her. "Step away from the console, Shalini," Kavya ordered, her voice steady. "It's over."

Shalini's eyes flicked around the room, calculating her chances of escape. Realizing she was outmatched; she slowly raised her hands in surrender. Kavya secured her and signalled the team that the target was in custody.

Back at TechSpySecure, Shalini was placed in a high-security interrogation room. Arjun and Kavya observed her through a one-way mirror, contemplating their next move. They needed her cooperation, but her loyalty to Phantom was a formidable barrier.

"She's our key to understanding Phantom's plans," Arjun said, turning to Kavya.

Kavya nodded. "I'll handle it. Let's see what we can get from her."

Entering the interrogation room, Kavya projected calm and authority. She knew intimidation wouldn't work with Shalini; she needed to appeal to her intellect and sense of self-preservation.

"Shalini," Kavya began, sitting across from her. "You're incredibly talented. You've achieved what most can only dream of. But working for Phantom—he sees you as expendable. Help us, and we can protect you. Use your skills for something greater."

Shalini's eyes flickered with a mix of defiance and uncertainty. "You don't know him," she retorted. "He's more than you can handle."

"Perhaps," Kavya conceded. "But we've come this far, and we're not stopping. Help us, and we can offer you a future, a chance to redefine your legacy."

The interrogation stretched on for hours, with Kavya slowly chipping away at Shalini's defenses. Meanwhile, Arjun and the team analyzed the data recovered from the facility, looking for any clues that might give them an edge.

Finally, Shalini began to crack. She revealed critical details about Phantom's operations—his methods, his next targets, and the vulnerabilities in his network. It was a goldmine of information, but Arjun knew it was just the beginning.

As they processed the new intel, the sense of urgency intensified. They had struck a significant blow, but the clock was ticking. Phantom was still out there, and his retaliation could be swift and brutal.

Arjun and Kavya stood side by side, reviewing the data. They had gained valuable insights, but the war was far from over. They needed to stay ahead, anticipate Phantom's next moves, and continue dismantling his network piece by piece.

The digital chess game continued, with each move bringing them closer to a final confrontation. As the shadows of betrayal and uncertainty loomed, Arjun and his team remained steadfast, ready to face whatever challenges lay ahead. The fight for cyber supremacy was relentless, but they were determined to emerge victorious.

In the heart of Mumbai, as the city pulsed with life, the guardians of TechSpySecure prepared for the next phase of their battle. United, driven by a common purpose, they were ready to confront the shadows in the dark. The war against Phantom was far from over, but Arjun and his team were ready to face it head-on, with unwavering resolve and a steadfast commitment to protecting their world from the unseen threats lurking in cyberspace.

****

CHAPTER 9

THE HONEYPOT TRAP

The mood in TechSpySecure headquarters was electric with tension and determination. The recent discovery of Raj's betrayal had rattled the team, and trust was a fragile thing. Yet, Arjun knew they couldn't afford to slow down. Shalini's information hinted at more sleeper agents embedded in critical infrastructures, and they needed a way to flush them out without tipping off Phantom.

Gathering the team in the command center, Arjun outlined their next move. "We're going to set a trap—a honeypot. We need to create a target so enticing that Phantom's operatives can't resist."

Kavya, always quick to think on her feet, nodded. "We'll need to build a fake database. Something that looks like it contains high-value data—financial secrets, government intelligence, anything Phantom would find irresistible."

Nisha added, "And we'll need to ensure we can trace any access attempts back to their source. I'll set up the monitoring protocols."

As the team dispersed to their tasks, Arjun's mind was a whirlwind of thoughts. They had to execute this perfectly; one slip-up could tip Phantom off and waste their only chance to identify the sleeper agents. The honeypot had to be convincing, and their tracking infallible.

Kavya and her team worked around the clock, crafting a highly detailed database. It was designed to mimic the layout and security protocols of genuine high-value targets. Nisha integrated sophisticated tracking systems, ensuring that any unauthorized access would trigger immediate alerts and precise location tracking.

Once everything was in place, they launched the honeypot, masking it as a careless leak by an insider at TechSpySecure on dark web forums frequented by cybercriminals. Now, it was a waiting game.

Hours passed, each tick of the clock amplifying the tension. The team monitored the network traffic with laser focus, eyes glued to the screens for any sign of activity. The atmosphere was thick with anticipation and anxiety.

Suddenly, Nisha's console beeped with a series of alerts. "We've got something," she announced, her voice cutting through the silence. "Someone's trying to breach the honeypot."

Arjun's eyes locked onto the screen. "Initiate the trace, Nisha. Let's see where this leads."

Kavya and Nisha worked in tandem, tracing the source of the breach. The attacker was skilled, using multiple layers of obfuscation to mask their location. But TechSpySecure's tracking protocols were robust, and slowly, they peeled back the layers.

"There," Kavya pointed to a map on the screen. "It's coming from an office building downtown. The 23rd floor."

Arjun's face hardened. "That's the headquarters of a major financial firm named Bandhan Finance. If Phantom has someone in there, they could cause serious damage."

The team moved quickly. Kavya led a tactical unit to the location while Arjun and Nisha stayed behind to coordinate the operation. They couldn't risk alerting the sleeper agent, so stealth was critical.

Kavya's team infiltrated the building seamlessly, blending in with the flow of employees leaving for the day. They made their way to the 23rd floor, navigating the maze of cubicles and offices under the cover of dusk.

Pinpointing the source of the breach to a corner office, Kavya signalled her team to surround the area. With swift precision, they breached the door, catching the lone figure inside off guard.

"Step away from the terminal," Kavya commanded, her voice cold and authoritative.

The man, visibly startled, raised his hands. "Who are you? What do you want?"

"We're here for you," Kavya replied, eyes locked on him. "And for the information you've been sending to Phantom."

Back at TechSpySecure, Arjun and Nisha watched the live feed from Kavya's bodycam. The man, identified as Sameer, a mid-level analyst at the financial firm, looked terrified but defiant.

"What did you find?" Arjun asked over the comms.

Kavya's voice came through steady. "He's been funnelling data through encrypted channels. We're pulling everything now."

Sameer's defiance turned to a mix of anger and fear as he was restrained. "You have no idea what you're up against," he spat. "Phantom is everywhere. You can't stop him."

Kavya's eyes hardened. "Watch us."

With Sameer in custody, they returned to TechSpySecure. The team began the painstaking task of sifting through the data he had been transmitting. It was a **trove** of information, detailing not only Phantom's operations but also revealing the identities of other sleeper agents.

As they pieced together the information, Arjun felt a mix of triumph and anxiety. They had struck a significant blow against Phantom, but this also meant Phantom would retaliate. The battle was far from over.

Gathered in the command center, the team debriefed. Meera's return had been a catalyst, and Sameer's data provided a clearer picture of Phantom's reach. But the revelation of more sleeper agents meant the threat was far from neutralized.

"This is a war of **attrition**," Arjun said, addressing his team. "Phantom will keep coming at us, and we need to stay one step ahead. Today, we've made significant progress, but we can't let our guard down this way."

Kavya nodded. "We'll continue to hunt down these agents. Phantom needs to know we're not backing down."

The team's resolve was stronger than ever. They were bruised but not broken, united by a common purpose. As they prepared for the next phase of their mission, the sense of camaraderie and determination was palpable. They were ready to confront whatever challenges lay ahead, driven by their commitment to protect their city and their world from the unseen threats that lurked in cyberspace.

Arjun knew the road ahead would be fraught with danger, but with his team by his side, he was confident they could face any challenge.

****

CHAPTER 10

UNRAVELING THE SLEEPERS

The air in TechSpySecure's command center was thick with anticipation. The capture of Sameer and the trove of data he'd been funnelling to Phantom had given Arjun and his team a renewed sense of purpose. But they also knew that with each step they took closer to dismantling Phantom's network, the danger increased exponentially.

Arjun gathered the team for a briefing. "We've identified several **sleeper agents** embedded within critical infrastructure sectors. Our next move is to neutralize these threats simultaneously. We need to coordinate with the authorities to ensure a seamless operation."

Kavya, laid out the plan. "We'll hit them at dawn when they least expect it. We need to move quickly and efficiently. Each team will target a specific location: power grids, financial institutions, and communication networks."

Nisha, deeply engrossed in decrypting the rest of Sameer's data, looked up. "We've also got intel on Phantom's next big move. They're planning a massive cyber-attack that could cripple the city. If we don't act now, the consequences will be catastrophic."

Arjun nodded. "This is it, then. We take down the sleeper agents and Phantom's plan. Everyone, gear up. We move out in one hour."

As the team prepared, Arjun took a moment to reflect on their journey. They had faced betrayals, uncovered deep conspiracies, and put their lives on the line. Yet, they stood undeterred, united by their mission.

The operation commenced with military precision. Teams deployed to various locations across the city, their movements synchronized to the second. Kavya led the assault on the power grid, while Nisha's team targeted the financial institutions. Arjun and a select group focused on the communication networks.

Kavya's team infiltrated the power grid facility, their presence a ghostly shadow in the pre-dawn light. They moved silently, disabling security systems and neutralizing guards with practiced efficiency. As they reached the control room, they found the sleeper agent, a technician named Ravi, attempting to sabotage the system.

"Step away from the console," Kavya ordered, her voice calm but firm.

Ravi turned, eyes wide with fear. "You can't stop us. Phantom is unstoppable."

Kavya approached him slowly. "We'll see about that." With a swift motion, she disarmed him and secured the control room.

Meanwhile, Nisha's team infiltrated a high-security financial building. The sleeper agent, a senior analyst named Priya, was in the process of transferring large sums of money to offshore accounts. Nisha's team moved quickly, isolating her in the server room.

"You're done, Priya," Nisha said, her voice carrying the weight of authority. "Step away from the terminal."

Priya's hands trembled as she raised them. "You have no idea what you're interfering with."

Nisha captured her and began the process of reversing the transactions, ensuring that no lasting damage was done.

Arjun's team faced a more complex challenge at the communication network hub. The sleeper agent here was highly skilled, having already begun to implement a malware attack that could disrupt emergency services and communications citywide.

As Arjun's team breached the facility, they encountered heavy resistance. The agent, identified as Suraj, was well-prepared and had fortified his position. A tense standoff ensued, with both sides exchanging fire.

Arjun moved with calculated precision, using cover to his advantage. "Suraj, give it up! You're outnumbered and outmatched."

Suraj, desperation etched on his face, replied, "You'll never stop Phantom. This is just the beginning."

With a coordinated effort, Arjun's team managed to flank Suraj, disarming him and securing the facility. They quickly moved to neutralize the malware and restore the network's integrity.

Back at TechSpySecure, the teams regrouped, bringing with them the captured sleeper agents. The atmosphere was charged with a mix of relief and anticipation. They had struck a significant blow against Phantom, but the real challenge was yet to come.

Meera, who had been working tirelessly alongside the team, approached Arjun. "There's something else you need to see," she said, her voice tinged with urgency.

In the command center, Meera pulled up a decrypted file from Sameer's data. It contained detailed plans for Phantom's ultimate attack—an all-out cyber assault designed to bring the city to its knees.

"This is it," Arjun said, his voice grim. "Phantom's endgame. We need to counteract this immediately."

Kavya, analysing the data, pointed out key weaknesses in Phantom's plan. "If we can exploit these vulnerabilities, we might be able to turn the tide."

Nisha added, "We'll need to coordinate with national cyber defence units. This is bigger than us."

Arjun nodded. "Contact the authorities. We'll need all the help we can get."

As TechSpySecure coordinated with government agencies, a plan was put into motion to intercept and neutralize Phantom's final assault. The city's cyber defences were bolstered, and emergency protocols were activated.

In the early hours of the morning, the assault began. Phantom unleashed a barrage of cyber-attacks, targeting critical infrastructure, financial systems, and communication networks. The city's digital landscape lit up with alerts and countermeasures.

Arjun, Kavya, Nisha, and Meera worked tirelessly, directing defence efforts and counter-attacks. The battle waged on for hours, each side pushing the other to the brink.

Finally, a breakthrough. Nisha, using a backdoor entry discovered in Sameer's data, managed to infiltrate Phantom's command and control server. "I've got access!" she shouted, her fingers dancing over the keyboard.

Arjun looked over, a glint of hope in his eyes. "Shut them down, Nisha. End this."

With precise keystrokes, Nisha unleashed a counter-attack, corrupting Phantom's control systems and severing their network links. One by one, the attacks ceased, the digital storm **abating**.

The command center erupted in cheers, the tension giving way to elation. They had done it. Phantom's assault had been thwarted.

Arjun addressed his team, his voice filled with pride and relief. "We faced the worst, and we prevailed. This victory is ours, but we must remain vigilant. Phantom's threat may be diminished, but it's not gone. We'll continue to protect and defend our city, no matter what."

As dawn broke over Mumbai, the city remained safe, its defenders standing strong against the shadows of cyber warfare. Arjun and his team knew the battle would continue, but they were ready, united by their mission and their unwavering resolve.

In the aftermath, as the team debriefed and celebrated their hard-fought victory, Arjun reflected on the journey. They had faced unimaginable challenges and emerged stronger; their bond unbreakable. The war against cyber threats was far from over, but with TechSpySecure leading the charge, the future looked brighter than ever.

****

CHAPTER 11

SHADOWS OF DECEPTION

With Phantom's primary assault thwarted, a semblance of normalcy returned to Mumbai. But Arjun and his team knew the calm was deceptive. Phantom was a hydra, with many heads waiting to strike back. In the days following their victory, TechSpySecure worked tirelessly to analyse the data from Sameer's files, uncovering more about Phantom's intricate web of deception.

In the command center, the atmosphere was one of cautious optimism. The screens were filled with lines of code and encrypted files, each a piece of the puzzle they were determined to solve.

Arjun stood at the center, his eyes scanning the room. "We've made significant progress, but we can't let our guard down. Phantom will regroup and come at us harder. We need to be ready."

Kavya, who had been cross-referencing the data, spoke up. "There's something peculiar here. Multiple references to an operation code-named 'Chimera'. It seems to be a fallback plan in case of failure."

Nisha joined in. "Chimera... It's mentioned in relation to several high-profile individuals and businesses. This could be Phantom's next big move."

Arjun nodded. "Then we need to figure out what Chimera is and neutralize it before they can implement it."

As the team delved deeper into the files, they discovered that Operation Chimera was an elaborate scheme designed to destabilize the economy by targeting key financial hubs and leveraging high-profile business leaders. It was a multi-faceted attack that would create chaos and undermine public trust.

Meera, who had been silently working on her laptop, suddenly looked up. "I've found something. There's a meeting scheduled for tonight at a high-end club downtown. The attendees include several names linked to Phantom."

Arjun's eyes narrowed. "This could be our chance to get ahead of them. We'll need to infiltrate the meeting and gather intel. Kavya, you're in charge of the **reconnaissance** team. Nisha, set up the surveillance."

The plan was set in motion. Kavya and a small team prepared for the infiltration, donning disguises to blend in with the elite crowd that frequented the club. Nisha rigged up a sophisticated array of surveillance equipment, ensuring they could monitor the meeting from a distance.

As night fell, the team moved into position. The club was a lavish venue, glittering with opulence and filled with Mumbai's elite. Kavya and her team mingled with the crowd, their eyes and ears trained on their targets.

Inside the VIP section, the meeting was already underway. High-profile business leaders and government officials were engaged in hushed conversations, their demeanour tense. Kavya, posing as a journalist, managed to get close enough to overhear snippets of their discussions.

"They're talking about Chimera," she whispered into her concealed microphone. "It's more advanced than we thought. They plan to use Artificial Intelligence algorithms to manipulate stock markets and launch a coordinated cyber-attack on financial institutions."

Arjun and Nisha, listening in from the command center, exchanged a look of urgency. "We need to act fast," Arjun said. "If they execute this plan, the fallout will be catastrophic."

Kavya continued to gather intel, her presence unnoticed amidst the glitz and glamour. But as she moved closer to the main group, one of the attendees, a sharp-eyed man in a tailored suit, seemed to recognize her. His eyes narrowed, and he signalled to security.

"Kavya, get out of there," Arjun's voice crackled through her earpiece. "You've been made."

Kavya nodded subtly and began to make her way towards the exit, maintaining her composure. But the sharp-eyed man had already alerted the club's security, and they were closing in.

Nisha quickly redirected the surveillance cameras to create a distraction. "I'm causing a power glitch in the main hall. It should give you a few seconds."

As the lights flickered and the music stuttered, Kavya seized the opportunity to slip through the confused crowd. She made her way to the back exit, where her team was waiting with a getaway car.

Back at TechSpySecure, the team reconvened, piecing together the information Kavya had gathered. They now had a clearer picture of Operation Chimera and its key players. The sharp-eyed man, identified as Rakesh Malhotra, was a senior executive at a major tech firm and a known associate of Phantom.

Arjun's mind raced as he formulated their next move. "We need to take down Rakesh and his network. If we can disrupt their coordination, we might be able to stop Chimera in its tracks."

The team prepared for a coordinated strike. They would hit multiple locations simultaneously, targeting Rakesh's associates and the tech infrastructure they planned to use for Chimera.

As dawn approached, TechSpySecure launched their operation. Teams moved with precision, raiding offices, seizing servers, and apprehending key figures. Rakesh, however, proved elusive. He had anticipated their move and gone underground.

Frustration mounted, but Arjun remained resolute. "We're close. We can't let him slip away."

Nisha, working tirelessly on tracking Rakesh's digital footprint, finally found a lead. "He's using a secure satellite link to communicate. If we can intercept it, we might trace his location."

Arjun and Nisha worked together, decoding the satellite link and pinpointing Rakesh's hideout. It was a villa on the outskirts of the city, heavily guarded and fortified.

Kavya, leading the tactical team, prepared for the assault. "We go in fast and quiet. Our priority is to capture Rakesh and gather any intel on Chimera."

The team moved in under the cover of night, breaching the villa's defences with swift efficiency. Inside, they found Rakesh and his closest associates, caught off guard by the sudden assault.

"Rakesh Malhotra," Kavya said, training her weapon on him. "It's over. You're coming with us."

Rakesh, cornered and defeated, sneered. "You think you've won? Phantom is bigger than any of us. You can't stop what's coming."

Kavya secured him, the weight of his words lingering in the air. They had struck a significant blow against Phantom, but the fight was far from over.

Back at TechSpySecure, as the sun rose over Mumbai, Arjun and his team sifted through the data recovered from Rakesh's hideout. They had foiled Operation Chimera, but the battle against Phantom would continue.

Arjun addressed his team, his voice filled with determination. "We've won this round, but the war is not over. Phantom is still out there, and we'll be ready for them. We'll protect our city, no matter what it takes."

United in their mission, TechSpySecure stood as the city's first line of defense against the shadows of cyber warfare, ready to face whatever challenges lay ahead.

****

CHAPTER 12

THE PHANTOM WITHIN

The sun was high over Mumbai, casting long shadows across headquarters. The team had barely had time to rest after the intense operation against Rakesh Malhotra. As they regrouped and reviewed the intel from Rakesh's hideout, a sense of foreboding settled over them. Despite their recent victory, the shadow of Phantom loomed large.

Arjun called an emergency meeting in the command center. "We've stopped Chimera, but Phantom's network is vast. Rakesh hinted at something bigger, something we haven't uncovered yet. We need to stay vigilant."

Kavya, her face set in determination, nodded. "Agreed. We need to go thorough into Rakesh's files. There has to be something we've missed."

Nisha, already at her terminal, started sifting through the data with renewed Vigor. "I'm running a deep analysis on the encrypted files. If there's a clue, we'll find it."

Hours turned into days as the team worked tirelessly. Each lead seemed to bring them closer to understanding Phantom's next move, but a crucial piece of the puzzle was still missing. Tensions ran high, and the strain was evident in the faces around the room.

One evening, as the team gathered for a briefing, Meera approached Arjun with a concerned look. "Arjun, there's something you need to see. It's from Rakesh's personal communications."

She handed him a tablet displaying a series of encrypted messages. As Arjun scanned through them, his eyes widened. "These are internal communications from TechSpySecure," he said, his voice heavy with disbelief. "Phantom has a mole within our team."

A stunned silence fell over the room. The realization that one of their own could be working against them was a blow to their morale. Arjun's mind raced as he considered the implications.

"We need to find the mole and fast," Kavya said, her voice breaking the silence. "If Phantom has someone on the inside, they'll know our every move."

Arjun nodded. "Agreed. We'll start by cross-referencing access logs with the times of critical breaches. Nisha, can you handle that?"

Nisha, already on her terminal, gave a quick nod. "On it. I'll run a thorough check on all recent activity."

As the team spread out to begin their investigation, Arjun couldn't shake the feeling of betrayal. They had faced so much together, and the thought that one of their own could be a traitor was almost too much to bear.

Hours later, Nisha called everyone back to the command center. "I've found something," she said, her voice tense.

"There's an unusual pattern in the access logs. Someone's been covering their tracks, but I managed to trace it back to one of us."

All eyes turned to the large screen where Nisha displayed the logs. The pattern was clear—sensitive data had been accessed at odd hours, always routed through a specific terminal.

Arjun's heart sank as he recognized the terminal's location. It belonged to Rajiv, one of their senior analysts and someone they had trusted implicitly. The team's shock was palpable.

"Rajiv?" Kavya said, her voice filled with disbelief. "It can't be."

Arjun clenched his fists. "We need to confront him. Now."

The team moved swiftly, making their way to Rajiv's office. They found him at his desk, seemingly engrossed in his work. When he saw the group approaching, his expression shifted from surprise to something unreadable.

"Rajiv, we need to talk," Arjun said, his voice firm.

Rajiv stood slowly, his eyes scanning the faces of his colleagues. "What's this about?"

"We know you've been accessing sensitive data and routing it to Phantom," Nisha said, her voice steady.

For a moment, Rajiv's face remained neutral. Then, a flicker of something—guilt, regret—crossed his features. "I can explain," he said quietly.

"Start talking," Kavya demanded.

Rajiv took a deep breath. "I didn't want to do it. They have my family. Phantom threatened to kill them if I didn't cooperate."

Arjun's anger flared. "Why didn't you come to us? We could have helped you."

"I didn't know who to trust," Rajiv replied, his voice breaking. "Phantom's reach is everywhere. I thought the only way to keep my family safe was to do what they asked."

The room fell silent as the weight of Rajiv's words sank in. They had all underestimated Phantom's ruthlessness.

"We need to get your family to safety," Arjun said finally. "And then we're going to take Phantom down once and for all."

Rajiv nodded, tears in his eyes. "I'm so sorry. I never wanted to betray you."

"We'll deal with this together," Kavya said, her voice softening. "But first, we need to get your family out of danger."

The team quickly devised a plan to extract Rajiv's family. Using their connections within law enforcement, they arranged for a discrete operation to relocate them to a safe house.

As they prepared for the extraction, Arjun gathered the team. "We're going to hit Phantom hard. Rajiv, you're going to help us. We need every bit of information you have."

Rajiv agreed, providing detailed insights into Phantom's operations and network. With his knowledge, they identified several key targets—safe houses, data centers, and communication hubs.

The extraction of Rajiv's family went off without a hitch, and they were safely relocated. With that weight lifted, the team focused on their next move.

Back in the command center, they mapped out a coordinated strike against Phantom's infrastructure. Each team member had a critical role to play, and the stakes had never been higher.

As they launched the operation, the air was thick with determination. Arjun led the charge, coordinating the assaults with precision. Teams moved in unison, hitting Phantom's assets simultaneously.

The battle was intense. Phantom's operatives fought back fiercely, but TechSpySecure's team was relentless. Rajiv's inside knowledge gave them the edge they needed, allowing them to anticipate Phantom's moves and counter them effectively.

Hours later, as the dust settled, TechSpySecure stood victorious. They had dismantled a significant portion of Phantom's network, captured key operatives and seized critical data.

Back at headquarters, the team gathered to debrief. There was a sense of accomplishment, but also a recognition that the fight was far from over.

Arjun addressed his team, his voice filled with pride and resolve. "Today, we struck a major blow against Phantom. But this is just the beginning. We'll continue to hunt them down, protect our city, and ensure that justice is served."

The team nodded in agreement; their bond stronger than ever. They knew the road ahead would be challenging, but they were ready to face whatever came their way.

As the sun set over Mumbai, casting a golden glow over the city, TechSpySecure stood as a beacon of hope in the battle against the shadows of cyber warfare. United in their mission, they were prepared to defend their city, no matter the cost.

****

CHAPTER 13

THE DARK WEB CONSPIRACY

The recent triumphs against Phantom had instilled a cautious optimism within TechSpySecure, but the looming presence of the cybercrime syndicate reminded them that their work was far from over. Phantom's tentacles reached deeper into the underbelly of the internet than they had anticipated, and the next challenge would test their limits.

Arjun stood in front of the large digital display in the command center, the blue light casting a glow over the room. Maps, diagrams, and lines of code covered the screen, outlining Phantom's known operations. "We've disrupted their immediate plans, but Phantom still has considerable resources at their disposal. Our next step is to dismantle their financial network. Without funding, their operations will cripple."

Kavya, ever the strategic mind, added, "We need to trace the flow of money through the dark web. It's where they launder their funds and procure their resources."

Nisha, focused intently on her terminal, interjected, "I've been monitoring the dark web chatter. There's a specific forum known as 'The Abyss' where Phantom's operatives frequently communicate. We might find our lead there."

Meera, who had become an invaluable asset to the team, nodded. "Gaining access to 'The Abyss' won't be easy. It's heavily encrypted and monitored by some of the best hackers in the world. We'll need to be careful."

Arjun, thinking strategically, said, "We need someone on the inside, someone who can blend in and gather information without raising suspicion."

Nisha looked up, determination in her eyes. "I can do it. I've got experience navigating these forums. But I'll need a secure connection and backup in case things go wrong."

Arjun agreed. "Alright, Nisha. You'll go in, but Kavya and Meera will monitor from here, ready to pull you out if necessary."

As Nisha prepared for her deep dive into the dark web, the rest of the team fortified their defences and set up the surveillance and a secure **VPN** for Nisha. The stress in the room was palpable.

Nisha took a deep breath, her fingers poised over the keyboard. With a final nod from Arjun, she began her descent into *'The Abyss.'* The screen in front of her filled with cryptic symbols and gateways, each requiring precise navigation to avoid detection.

After what felt like hours, Nisha finally gained access to the forum. It was a **labyrinth** of hidden messages and coded language, but her expertise allowed her to decode the critical information. She found a thread discussing a massive transfer of funds set to occur within the next 48 hours. The transaction was encrypted and hidden across multiple **cryptocurrencies** and accounts.

"Kavya, Meera, I've found something. They're planning to move a huge amount of money soon. This could be our chance to trace it back to their source."

Meera analysed the data on her screen. "We need to intercept this transaction. If we can follow the money trail, we might find their financial backbone."

Arjun, pacing behind them, strategized. "We need to set up a digital sting operation. Nisha, can you plant a tracker in the transaction?"

Nisha's fingers flew across the keyboard. "Already on it. I'm embedding a stealth tracker in the transaction code. It will lead us to the recipient accounts without being detected."

The team watched as Nisha completed the task, holding their breath. The next 48 hours would be critical. They needed to monitor the transaction and trace the funds to their ultimate destination.

As the transaction went live, the team worked in shifts, ensuring round-the-clock surveillance. The trail led them through a maze of digital wallets, offshore accounts, and cryptocurrency exchanges. It was an exhausting process, but they were relentless.

Finally, the trail led to a seemingly **innocuous** company registered in a tax haven. But as Meera dug deeper, she uncovered that the company was a front for Phantom's financial operations.

Arjun gathered the team. "We've got them. This company is the main source of their funding. If we can take it down, we'll deal a severe blow to Phantom."

Kavya suggested, "We need to coordinate with international law enforcement. This operation spans multiple jurisdictions, and we'll need their cooperation."

Arjun agreed. "Meera, set up a secure line with our contacts in INTERPOL and the financial crime units. We're going to need all the help we can get."

The next few days were a whirlwind of activity. TechSpySecure worked with international agencies to freeze the accounts and dismantle the financial network. The operation was complex, involving legal manoeuvres and cyber tactics, but their preparation paid off.

As the international task force moved in, Phantom's financial empire crumbled. The operation was a resounding success, leading to the arrest of several high-ranking Phantom operatives and the seizure of millions in assets.

Back at TechSpySecure, the team celebrated their victory. They had struck a major blow against Phantom, crippling their ability to fund future operations. The mood was jubilant, but they knew their work wasn't done.

Arjun addressed the team, his voice filled with pride and determination. "We've won a significant battle, but the war continues. Phantom is weakened, but they're not defeated. We need to stay vigilant and be ready for their next move."

Kavya, smiling, added, "And we will be. We've proven that when we work together, we're unstoppable."

As the team raised their glasses in a toast to their victory, they knew that the road ahead would still be fraught with challenges. But united by their mission and strengthened by their bond, they were ready to face whatever came their way.

****

CHAPTER 14

THE FINAL RECKONING

The morning sun was just beginning to light up the Mumbai skyline as Arjun called an early meeting. The team gathered in the command center, the air thick with anticipation.

"Phantom is wounded but not defeated," Arjun began, his tone serious. "We need to anticipate their next move. We've dealt a severe blow to their finances, but that means they'll be desperate and unpredictable."

Kavya nodded. "We need to be ready for anything. Desperation can lead them to make bold, reckless decisions."

Nisha, always the analytical mind, added, "I've been monitoring dark web activity. There's been a spike in encrypted communications that could be Phantom rallying their remaining forces."

Meera, who had been working on a separate terminal, suddenly looked up. "I've found something. There's chatter about a major cyber-attack planned for the end of the week. The target isn't clear yet, but the scale suggests something catastrophic."

Arjun's eyes narrowed. "We need to find out what they're planning and stop it before they can execute it."

The team split up, each member diving into their specific tasks. Nisha and Meera focused on decrypting the communications, while Kavya and Rajiv, who had fully regained the team's trust, worked on tracing the origins of the messages.

Hours turned into days as they pieced together the clues. The breakthrough came when Nisha cracked the final layer of encryption, revealing a detailed plan: Phantom was targeting Mumbai's , Borivali's critical infrastructure, aiming to bring the city to a standstill.

"They're planning a multi-pronged attack," Nisha explained, pulling up the detailed plans. "Power grids, water supply, transportation systems – everything. If they succeed, it will be chaos."

Arjun's face was set with determination. "We need to counteract their moves at every point. We'll set up defences around each target and prepare for rapid response. This is going to be the final showdown."

The team mobilized, coordinating with city officials and emergency services to fortify the critical infrastructure. They also established a central command post where they could monitor and respond to any attacks in real-time.

The night before the planned attack, the team gathered one last time to review their strategy. Tensions were high, but the bond between them was unbreakable.

"We've come a long way," Arjun said, looking around at his team. "No matter what happens tomorrow, know that I'm proud of each and every one of you. We're going to stop Phantom and protect our city."

The following day, the attack began as expected. Phantom unleashed a sophisticated, coordinated assault on Mumbai's infrastructure. Power grids were targeted with advanced malware, water supply systems were hacked, and the transportation network was disrupted with DDoS attacks.

But TechSpySecure was ready. Arjun and his team responded swiftly, countering each attack with precision. Kavya led the defences of the power grids, deploying countermeasures that neutralized the malware. Nisha and Meera worked together to restore the water supply systems, isolating the affected segments and rerouting control to secure servers.

Rajiv, using his inside knowledge of Phantom's tactics, played a crucial role in defending the transportation network. His quick thinking and expertise allowed them to fend off the **DDoS attacks** and restore communication between control centers.

Despite their best efforts, Phantom managed to breach several systems, causing temporary blackouts and disruptions. But the team's rapid response minimized the impact, and they quickly regained control.

As the day wore on, the intensity of the attacks increased. Phantom was throwing everything they had left, desperate to achieve their goal. But TechSpySecure & Cyber Squad held the line, their coordinated efforts proving too formidable for Phantom to overcome.

In the command center, Arjun coordinated the defences, his voice calm but commanding. "Stay focused. We're almost through this."

Hours later, as the sun set over Mumbai, the attacks began to wane. Phantom's resources were depleted, and their operatives were either captured or in retreat. TechSpySecure had won the battle.

The city slowly returned to normal, with power restored, water flowing, and transportation systems back online. The team gathered in the command center, exhausted but victorious.

Arjun looked at his team, a sense of pride and relief washing over him. "We did it. We stopped them."

Kavya smiled with a sense of love towards Arjun, a rare sight after the intense days they had endured. "This was our toughest battle yet, but we came through."

Nisha nodded. "Phantom is finished. They've lost their resources, their operatives, and their ability to cause chaos."

Rajiv, who had redeemed himself with his crucial contributions, said quietly, "Thank you for trusting me. I'm proud to be part of this team."

Arjun placed a hand on Rajiv's shoulder. "We couldn't have done it without you, Rajiv. We're all part of this victory."

As the team celebrated their hard-earned triumph, they knew that their work was far from over. The world of cyber warfare was ever-evolving, and new threats would inevitably arise. But TechSpySecure was ready, united by their mission and strengthened by their victories.

Standing together in the command center, they looked out over the city they had sworn to protect. They were the guardians of Mumbai's digital frontier, always vigilant, always ready.

****

CHAPTER 15

THE AFTERMATH

The aftermath of the battle against Phantom left a city and a team both weary and wary. While TechSpySecure had emerged victorious, the scars of the conflict ran deep, both in the digital realm and in the hearts of those who had fought on the front lines.

As Mumbai began to recover from the chaos unleashed by Phantom's attacks, Arjun and his team turned their focus inward, assessing the toll the conflict had taken on their own ranks. They had faced danger, betrayal, and uncertainty, and now they needed time to heal.

Arjun called for a meeting in the command center, not to strategize or plan their next move, but to check in on each other, to offer support and solidarity in the wake of their shared ordeal.

"Before we can move forward," Arjun began, his voice steady but tinged with fatigue, "we need to take care of ourselves and each other. This battle has taken its toll, and it's important that we give ourselves time to heal."

Kavya nodded in agreement. "We've been through a lot, but we're stronger together. Let's make sure we're there for each other as we process what we've been through."

Nisha, who had spent countless hours poring over code and data during the conflict, added, "It's okay to not be okay. We've faced some unimaginable challenges, and it's normal to need time to recover."

Meera, who had been a pillar of strength throughout the ordeal, spoke up. "We've proven that we can overcome anything when we stand together. Let's lean on each other as we navigate the aftermath of this battle."

Rajiv, who had faced his own demons and emerged stronger for it, said quietly, "Thank you for giving me a second chance. I won't forget what you've done for me."

Arjun smiled, a glimmer of hope shining through the exhaustion. "We're a team, through thick and thin. We'll get through this together, just like we always do."

In the days that followed, TechSpySecure focused on rebuilding not just the city's infrastructure, but also their own resilience and camaraderie. They took time to rest, to recharge, and to reconnect with loved ones who had stood by them during the darkest days. As Mumbai returned to a semblance of normalcy, Arjun and his team knew that their work was far from over. The world of cybersecurity was ever-changing, and new threats would inevitably arise. But they were ready, united by their shared experiences and strengthened by their bonds of friendship and trust.

And as they looked out over the city they had sworn to protect, they knew that no matter what challenges lay ahead, they would face them together, as the guardians of Mumbai's digital frontier.

CHAPTER 16

NEW HORIZONS

With the dust settled from the conflict with Phantom and Mumbai on the path to recovery, TechSpySecure found themselves at a crossroads. The battles they had fought had forged them into a formidable team, but they knew that their work was far from over. As they looked to the future, new challenges and opportunities awaited.

Arjun called for a meeting in the command center, a sense of determination in his eyes. "We've faced some of our toughest challenges together, and we've emerged stronger for it. But we can't afford to rest on our laurels. There are still threats out there, waiting to be uncovered."

Kavya nodded, her mind already racing with possibilities. "We need to stay one step ahead of the hackers. That means investing in cutting-edge technology, training our team to adapt to new threats, and forging alliances with other cybersecurity experts."

Nisha, always the **pragmatist**, added, "We also need to be proactive in identifying potential threats before they materialize. That means strengthening our intelligence-gathering capabilities and monitoring the dark web for any signs of trouble."

Meera, who had proven herself to be a formidable asset in both the technical and strategic realms, suggested, "We should also focus on raising awareness among the public about cybersecurity best practices. The more people are educated about the risks, the less vulnerable they'll be to attacks."

Rajiv, who had earned back the trust of his teammates through his actions during the conflict with Phantom, spoke up. "And we shouldn't forget about our own team. We need to prioritize their well-being and professional development. Happy and fulfilled employees are the best defence against burnout and turnover."

Arjun smiled, a sense of pride swelling within him. "I couldn't agree more. Together, we've faced down some of the most dangerous threats the digital world has to offer. And as long as we continue to work together, there's nothing we can't accomplish."

As the team dispersed, each member filled with a renewed sense of purpose and determination, Arjun allowed himself a moment of quiet reflection. The road ahead would undoubtedly be challenging, but with his team by his side, he knew they were ready to face whatever came their way.

And as the sun set over Mumbai, casting long shadows across the cityscape, TechSpySecure stood ready to confront the future, united in their mission to protect and defend, no matter the cost.

****

CHAPTER 17

THE UNFORESEEN THREAT

In the weeks following their victory over Phantom and amidst their preparations for future challenges, TechSpySecure found themselves facing an unexpected adversary. It came in the form of a seemingly innocuous email, one that slipped past their defences unnoticed.

Arjun, Kavya, Nisha, Meera, and Rajiv were gathered in the command center, discussing their latest security protocols and potential vulnerabilities. As they delved into the intricacies of their systems, an urgent notification flashed on Nisha's screen.

"What's this?" Nisha muttered, her brow furrowing in concern. "I've intercepted a suspicious email. It bypassed our filters and encryption protocols."

Kavya leaned in, studying the contents of the email. "It looks like a routine message, but something feels off about it."

Arjun, ever vigilant, ordered, "Run a thorough analysis. We can't afford to take any chances."

Nisha worked quickly, dissecting the email's code and attachments with precision. As she dug deeper, her expression grew graver.

"This isn't just any email," Nisha announced, her voice tense. "It's a sophisticated **phishing** attempt, designed to infiltrate our network and steal sensitive data."

Meera's eyes widened in alarm. "Could it be Phantom? Have they regrouped and launched a new offensive?"

Rajiv, who had been monitoring their systems for any signs of intrusion, shook his head. "It's too early to say. But whoever sent this email is well-versed in cyber deception."

Arjun's jaw tightened with determination. "We need to shut down this threat before it can do any damage. Nisha, can you trace the source?"

Nisha nodded, her fingers flying across the keyboard. "I'm tracing the IP address now. It's bouncing through multiple proxies, but I think I can pinpoint the origin."

As Nisha worked to track down the source of the phishing attempt, the rest of the team sprang into action. Kavya mobilized their defences, tightening security protocols and deploying additional firewalls to safeguard their systems. Meera reached out to their contacts in law enforcement and cybersecurity agencies, alerting them to the potential threat.

Hours passed as the team worked tirelessly to neutralize the phishing attempt and trace its origins. Finally, Nisha's efforts paid off.

"I've located the source," Nisha announced, relief evident in her voice. "It's a rogue hacker operating out of a remote location. I'm sending the coordinates to our contacts in law enforcement."

Arjun nodded in approval. "Good work, Nisha. Let's shut this down before it can escalate any further."

With the authorities alerted to the threat, TechSpySecure focused on fortifying their defences and educating their staff about the dangers of phishing attacks. They conducted regular training sessions, teaching employees how to recognize and respond to suspicious emails, and implemented stringent verification processes to prevent unauthorized access to their systems.

In the end, the phishing attempt was thwarted, and the rogue hacker apprehended. But the incident served as a sobering reminder that the threats they faced were ever-present and evolving. As they looked to the future, Arjun and his team knew that their work was far from over. But they were ready to face whatever challenges came their way, united in their mission to protect and defend, no matter the cost.

****

CHAPTER 18

THE CYBER ARMS RACE

TechSpySecure had emerged victorious from their encounter with the rogue hacker, but the incident had left them acutely aware of the ever-evolving landscape of cyber threats. As they continued to fortify their defences and educate their staff, a new challenge emerged on the horizon: a surge in cyber-attacks orchestrated by state-sponsored adversaries.

Arjun and his team were gathered in the command center, analysing the latest data on cyber-attacks targeting critical infrastructure and government institutions. The frequency and sophistication of the attacks were unprecedented, and it was clear that TechSpySecure was facing a formidable opponent.

Nisha, who had been monitoring the dark web for any signs of activity, spoke up. "The chatter on the dark web suggests that these attacks are part of a coordinated effort by state-sponsored hackers. They're targeting everything from power grids to financial systems, with the goal of destabilizing the region."

Kavya's expression was grim as she processed the implications. "If these attacks continue unchecked, the consequences could be catastrophic. We need to find a way to counter-attack them before they can inflict serious damage."

Meera, who had been in contact with government agencies and international cybersecurity organizations, added, "We're not alone in this fight. Our allies are mobilizing their resources to track down the perpetrators and neutralize the threat."

Rajiv, ever the realist, cautioned, "We need to be prepared for the possibility that these attacks will escalate. Our adversaries are well-funded and highly skilled, and they won't hesitate to use every tool at their disposal to achieve their objectives."

Arjun nodded in agreement. "We need to stay one step ahead of them. That means strengthening our defences, enhancing our intelligence-gathering capabilities, and collaborating closely with our allies."

As the team delved deeper into their analysis, they uncovered evidence of a looming cyber arms race. State-sponsored hackers were developing increasingly sophisticated malware and exploiting previously unknown vulnerabilities in their quest for dominance in the digital realm.

With each passing day, the stakes grew higher, and the pressure on TechSpySecure intensified. But Arjun and his team were undaunted. They knew that the future of cybersecurity depended on their ability to adapt and innovate in the face of adversity.

****

CHAPTER 19

THE GUARDIANS UNITE

In the wake of the escalating cyber threats and the ever-present spectre of state-sponsored attacks, TechSpySecure knew that they couldn't fight this battle alone. They needed to forge alliances, both within their own city and with cybersecurity experts around the globe.

Arjun and his team reached out to their counterparts in other cities, sharing intelligence, resources, and strategies for combating cyber threats. They collaborated on joint exercises and simulations, testing their defenses against simulated attacks and honing their skills in real-time.

At the same time, TechSpySecure established partnerships with international cybersecurity organizations and government agencies, pooling their expertise and coordinating their efforts to track down and neutralize the **perpetrators** behind the attacks.

The cyber arms race raged on, but TechSpySecure was not alone in their fight. They were part of a global network of defenders, united in their mission to protect and defend against cyber threats wherever they may arise.

As the years passed, the cyber landscape continued to evolve, presenting new challenges and opportunities for innovation. But through it all, TechSpySecure remained steadfast in their commitment to safeguarding their city and its citizens from the dangers of the digital world.

And so, as the sun set over Mumbai, casting a warm glow over the bustling streets below, Arjun and his team stood united, ready to face whatever the future held. For they were not just defenders of the digital realm, but guardians of a brighter, safer tomorrow for all.

A suspicious link found by the team when Arjun was going through the flashback history of the case from the start to find certain clue or any loophole or something which is missing. On analysing the whole case till now, they found that Phantom too was one of the main piece in this game of chess but not the king to whom they can checkmate. The actual mastermind is yet to be traced.

****

CHAPTER 20

THE MASTERMIND

A sense of unease settled over Arjun and his team as they processed the revelation that Phantom had been merely a pawn in a larger game, orchestrated by a mysterious figure known only as "The Architect." Their victory over Phantom felt hollow in the face of this new revelation, and the shadow of uncertainty loomed larger than ever before.

Arjun and Kavya found themselves once again at the heart of the storm, their relationship tested by the weight of their responsibilities and the looming threat of The Architect's grand design. They had weathered many storms together, but this new challenge tested the limits of their love and dedication.

As they delved deeper into the mystery of The Architect's identity and motives, they uncovered a tangled web of deceit and manipulation, stretching across borders and through the corridors of power. The Architect's ultimate plan remained elusive, shrouded in secrecy and obscured by layers of deception.

But Arjun and Kavya were not alone in their quest to uncover the truth. With the support of their team at TechSpySecure, they embarked on a relentless pursuit of answers, following every lead and leaving no stone unturned in their search for the elusive mastermind.

As the days turned into weeks, and the weeks into months, the threat posed by The Architect grew ever more ominous. Rumours circulated of impending cyber-attacks on a global scale, hinting at the architect's ultimate goal: chaos on an unprecedented level.

But amidst the uncertainty and fear, Arjun and Kavya found strength in each other, their love and dedication serving as a beacon of hope in the darkest of times. Together, they faced the unknown with courage and resolve, ready to confront whatever challenges lay ahead whether it is laid by Phantom or by the architect.

As they prepared for the inevitable showdown with The Architect, they knew that their journey was far from over. The stakes were higher than ever before, and the fate of not just Mumbai, but the world itself, hung in the balance.

And so, as the sun set over the city skyline, casting long shadows across the streets below, Arjun and Kavya stood ready to confront the mastermind behind it all. For they knew that no matter what the future held, they would face it together, united in their love and dedication to each other and to the city they called home.

****

EPILOGUE: THE LEGACY OF CYBER SHADOWS

In the ever-shifting landscape of the digital world, where shadows lurk in the depths of the internet and threats loom unseen behind screens, there emerges a beacon of hope: TechSpySecure. Their journey, chronicled in these pages, has been one of triumph and tribulation, of victories won and challenges overcome. From their humble beginnings to their rise as guardians of Mumbai's digital frontier, Arjun and his team have faced down adversaries both human and virtual, their resolve unyielding, their spirit unbroken.

But their story is not just one of battles fought and won. It is a testament to the power of unity, of teamwork, and of the unwavering commitment to a cause greater than oneself. It is a reminder that in the face of darkness, there is always light, and that even in the direst of circumstances, hope can prevail.

As the final pages of this book turn, let us not forget the lessons learned and the sacrifices made. Let us remember that the fight against cyber threats is ongoing, and that the legacy of TechSpySecure lives on in all those who strive to protect and defend in the digital age.

And so, as we close these chapters of their story, let us look to the future with optimism and determination. For though the shadows may linger, we know that there are those who stand ready to face them, armed with courage, conviction, and the unwavering belief that together, we can build a safer, more secure world for all.

Until then stay safe and stay secure and be vigilant towards cybercrimes and cybersecurity.

****

GLOSSARY

Encryption: Process of encoding information, which is conversion of the original representation of the information, known as plaintext, into an alternative form known as ciphertext.

Obfuscation: Intentionally confusing wording to confuse people apart from an intended audience.

Proxy Sever: In computer networking, a proxy server is a server application that acts as an intermediary between a client requesting a resource and the server providing that resource.

Social Engineering: Social engineering is the act of influencing a person to take an action that may or may not be in their best interest. It is a psychological manipulation technique used to trick individuals into divulging confidential information, performing certain actions, or gaining unauthorized access to systems or networks.

Penetration testing, also known as pen testing or ethical hacking, is a security exercise where a cyber-security expert attempts to find and exploit vulnerabilities in a computer system.

IP Address: An Internet Protocol address (IP address) is a numerical label such as 192.0.2.1 that is assigned to a device connected to a computer network that uses the Internet Protocol for communication. IP addresses serve two main functions: network interface identification, and location addressing.

Ambush: A sudden attack made from a concealed position.

Audacious: extremely bold or fearless.

Honeypot Security: Honeypot security is a computer security mechanism designed to detect, deflect, or counteract attempts at unauthorized use of information systems. It consists of data or systems that appear to be a legitimate part of the site, containing valuable information or resources, but are actually decoys or traps for attackers. The goal of honeypot security is to monitor and analyse the behaviour of attackers, gather intelligence on their tactics, and improve the organization's security posture.

Fanaticism: Belief or behaviour involving uncritical zeal or an obsessive enthusiasm.

Assault: An assault is the illegal act of causing physical harm or unwanted physical contact to another person, or, in some legal definitions, the threat or attempt to do so. It is both a crime and a tort and, therefore, may result in criminal prosecution, civil liability, or both.

Onslaught: A sudden and onset of trouble or a very powerful attack.

Chessboard: A chessboard is a game board used to play chess. It consists of 64 squares, 8 rows by 8 columns, on which the chess pieces are placed. It is square in shape and uses two colours of squares, one light and one dark, in a chequered pattern.

Espoinage: The practice of spying or of using spies to obtain secret information, especially regarding a government or business.

Trojan Horse: In computing, a Trojan horse (or simply Trojan) is any malware that misleads users of its true intent by disguising itself as a standard program.

Trove: A trove of information refers to a valuable and abundant collection of knowledge, data, or facts that are often hidden, discovered, or uncovered.

Attrition: A gradual reduction in number or strength because of stress or military action.

Sleeper Agent: A sleeper agent is a spy or operative who is placed in a target country or organization, not to undertake an immediate mission, but instead to act as a potential asset on short notice if activated.

Abating: To reduce in amount, degree or intensity.

Reconnaissance: An examination of a region for the purpose of gathering information of enemy's territory or region.

Deception: Deception is the act of convincing one or many recipients of untrue information. The person creating the deception knows it to be false while the receiver of the message has a tendency to believe it (although it's not always the case). It is often done for personal gain or advantage.

VPN (Virtual Private Network): VPN is a mechanism for creating a secure and private connection between a computing device and a computer network, or between two networks, using an insecure communication medium such as the public Internet. In simpler terms, a VPN is a service that encrypts your internet traffic and protects your online identity.

Labyrinth: A system of narrow corridors designed to confuse those who enter and make finding a correct path difficult.

Cryptocurrencies: A cryptocurrency, crypto-currency, or crypto[a] is a digital currency designed to work as a medium of exchange through a computer network that is not reliant on any central authority, such as a government or bank, to uphold or maintain it.

Innocuous: harmless, innocent, safe and inoffensive.

DDoS attacks: Distributed Denial of Service Attack is a cyber attack disrupting service by overloading the provider of the service.

Pragmatist: One who acts in a practical or straightforward manner; one who is pragmatic; one who values practicality or pragmatism.

Phishing: Phishing is a type of fraudulent practice where an attacker pretends to be a reputable entity or person in an email, text message, or other form of communication. The goal is to trick the recipient into revealing sensitive information, such as login credentials, financial information, or other personal data. Types of Phishing: *Email Phishing, Spear Phishing, Whaling.*

Perpetrators: a person who perpetrates, or commits, an illegal, criminal, or evil act.

ACKNOWLEDGEMENTS

My sincere thanks to almighty, Waheguru for helping me through some trying months and take the most important decisions of my life.

I would like to thank the divine energy inside my soul that pushes me to write. I thank my late grandfather S. Parkash Singh ji for helping me and supporting my education and daily needs.

I also like to thank my sister – Mrs. Lovenoor Kaur for being a support hand at every step of my life and my parents - S. Sukhwinderjit Singh, PES(A), Ex-Lecturer Chemistry & Sardarni (Mrs.) Gurdeep Kaur, Lecturer Chemistry; for making me this much capable.

I would also like to thank my uncle Bhupinder Shahi and for being light of inspiration. I would also like to thank to this technological era of Artificial Intelligence which helped a lot in bringing the years of work into months.

I would also like to thank the south Indian film industry for creating the films on hacking and movies with extra thriller for providing excellent references of the chapters in this book.

Also, I would like to thank my relatives, teachers and friends who directly or indirectly helped me during this journey.

Thank you all!

ER. HEM INDER SINGH